1 MONTH OF
FREE
READING

at
www.ForgottenBooks.com

By purchasing this book you are eligible for one month membership to ForgottenBooks.com, giving you unlimited access to our entire collection of over 1,000,000 titles via our web site and mobile apps.

To claim your free month visit:
www.forgottenbooks.com/free791976

ISBN 978-0-483-61765-0
PIBN 10791976

For support please visit www.forgottenbooks.com

VOL. II. JULY, 1881. No. 10.

The Glory of God is Intelligence.

THE

CONTRIBUTOR.

A MONTHLY MAGAZINE

REPRESENTING THE

YOUNG MEN'S AND YOUNG LADIES' MUTUAL IMPROVEMENT ASSOCIATIONS
OF THE LATTER-DAY SAINTS.

EDITED AND PUBLISHED BY JUNIUS F. WELLS.

SALT LAKE CITY, UTAH.

OFFICE: 15 EAST TEMPLE STREET, FIRST DOOR NORTH OF Z. C. M. I.

THE CONTRIBUTOR.

CONTENTS FOR JULY, 1881.

THE CONTRIBUTOR.

The Glory of God is Intelligence.

VOL. II.   JULY, 1881.   NO. 10.

DIVINE ORIGIN OF THE BOOK OF MORMON.

IV.

HISTORICAL EVIDENCES CONSIDERED.

IN the preceding number we traced the historic migrations, from the old to the new world, of Votan and the seven families whom he led by divine command to this continent. We likewise made brief extracts from the Book of Mormon, showing that a similar commandment had been given by the Lord to the brother of Jared, who led, under divine instruction, a small colony to America. The two accounts evidently refer to the same persons and circumstances; the account of the peregrinations of the one colony being almost, if not entirely, identical with the other. In this number we desire to make further comparisons, and to briefly note the historical account of this remarkable character and founder of the Votanic dynasty, under which the first peopling of America was accomplished.

"The achievements of Votan in the new world were as great as any of the heroes of antiquity. His great city, named Nachan (city of the serpents), from his own race, which was named Chan, a serpent. This Nachan is unquestionably identified with Palenque." De Bourbourg fixes the founding of this city shortly after the journeyings of Votan, 1000 B. C.; while Garcia Pelaez states that Votan founded Culhuacan, or Palenque, in the year 3000 of the world.

"The kingdom of the serpents flourished so rapidly that Votan founded three tributary monarchies, whose capitals were Tulan, Mayapan, and Chiquimula. The former is supposed to have been sit-

uated about two leagues east of the town of Ococingo; Mayapan is well known to have been the capital of Yucatan, and Chiquimula is thought to have been Copan, in Honduras. * * Votan deposited a great treasure at Huehuetan, in Soconusco, which he left under the vigilant care of a guard directed by one of the most honorable women of the land. Finally, he wrote a book in which he recorded his deeds and offered proof of his being a Chane (or serpent.) This ancient document, which is claimed to have been written by one of Votan's descendants, of the eighth or ninth generation, and not by himself, was in the Tzendal language, a dialect or branch of the Maya, spoken in Chiapas and around Palenque. Its history is, however, quite checkered, and the information which it contained comes very indirectly. For generations the Votanic document was scrupulously guarded by the people of Tacoalya, in Soconusco, but was finally discovered by Francisco Nuñez de la Vega, bishop of Chiapas. In the preamble of his *Constituciones,* sec. xxx, he claims to have read this document, but it is probable that only a copy, still in the Tzendal language but written in Latin characters, had come into his possession. He fails to give any definite information from the document except the most general statements with reference to Votan's place in the calendar, and his having seen the Tower of Babel, at which each people was given a new language. He states that he could have made more revelations of the history of Votan from this document but for bringing up the old idolatry of the people and perpetuating it. With the zeal of a true Vandal, the bishop committed the dangerous documents, together with the treasure which he claims Votan to have buried in the dark-house, to the flames in 1691. There seems to have been other copies, however, of this remarkable manuscript, for about the close of the eighteenth century, Dr. Paul Felix Cabrera was shown a document in the possession of Don Ramon de Ordoñez y Aguiar, a resident of Ciudad Real in Chiapas, which purported to be the Votanic memoir."—Short, pp. 205-7.

In connection with this brief extract there are several important points which demand the careful attention of the reader. First, let us consider the evident ruling desire of Votan to perpetuate, in his own name, and in that of the capital city of the extensive empire founded by him, the greatness and glory typified by a serpent; which, throughout the entire history of the Quichés, Olemecs, Toltecs or Nahua races, is found to be an emblem of power. The vivifying force in nature, "the god of the harvest and of the air," "the vapor clouds and vernal showers with their refreshing and fructifying influences," giving life, light and being—a deity as personified by Quetzalcoatl among the Nahuas, Gucumatz among the Quichés, and Cukulcan among the Mayas, each meaning, when translated, identically the same thing, namely, "feathered," or "plumed," or "winged" serpent.

When Moses led the children of Israel from bondage into the wilderness, we learn that they were on a certain occasion grievously afflicted by fiery serpents, whose bite inflicted death. God, however, commanded Moses to make a serpent of brass, and to lift it up upon a pole, in the midst of the people, so that all who had been bitten might be healed through the exercise of faith prompting obedience to the commandment requiring them to look upon the brazen serpent which was lifted up, that they might not perish. In this we find represented the death wrought by Satan in the Garden of Eden, when our parents yielded to the

temptation of the serpent; and we also have typified the lifting up, or crucifixion of the Savior. So that, as in the wilderness, those who were bitten unto death had life again, by looking up to the emblem which was raised in their midst to secure their temporal salvation; so, in like manner, all who die from the effects of the bite inflicted by the serpent upon Adam shall live again through the atoning blood and redeeming power of Jesus.

With this view, it would hardly seem reasonable to suppose that Votan, who had led a colony from Babel to this land, had written a book to prove that he was the descendant, or the representative of the powers or excellencies of an ordinary serpent, or common reptile. He, having acted under divine command, is it not far more reasonable and consistent, and more in harmony with the leading idea of the primitive inhabitants of the continent, that he sought to perpetuate, in his own name, and in the name of his great capital, the healing, redeeming, revivifying, characteristic powers of Christ Jesus our Lord?

Recent explorations, by Charnay, at Palenque go far to prove that it was built, if not entirely, almost wholly as a city of worship—a place for the performance of religious ordinances and ceremonies. When we consider this fact in connection with the testimony already herein given of the bishop of Chiapas, "that he could have made more revelations of the history of Votan from this document but for bringing up the old idolatry of the people and perpetuating it," we can readily understand that Votan was not only a hero, an empire founder, a great leader, but was more than all these—a deeply religious character. As to what the early Catholic bishops and clergy were pleased to consider the *idolatry* of the Indians at the time of the Spanish conquest of Mexico and Peru, we need only mention how they endeavored to account for the remarkable knowledge, with which they found the primitive inhabitants familiar, pertaining to Jewish laws, customs and ceremonies, and pertaining to the Gospel plan of human redemption, namely, "that the devil, seeing the effects of these things on the inhabitants of the old world, sought to, and had *counterfeited* them in the new." Men who could manifest such a high order of inventive credulity, would not be likely to prove slow in pronouncing the belief and practice of others idolatrous, though they might, in every particular, agree with that enjoined by the law and the Gospel. Be this, however, as it may, we find no reason for believing that De la Vega ever had in his possession either the treasure of Votan or the book written by him; though he may have had, and undoubtedly did have one written by some of the primitive historians many centuries later; which doubtless contained a transcript of some of the truths contained in the original Votanic document. The value of the treasure and writings of this great follower of the Divine voice is evidenced by the fact of their having been so carefully guarded for so many generations.

We will now turn to the Book of Mormon in search of clearer light upon this interesting subject; after which we shall leave the reader to draw his own conclusions as to whether or not Votan and the brother of Jared were identical. We have already seen, as shown in a previous article, that the former led, by divine command, a small colony, whose language was not confounded, from the great Tower to America, and that the brother of Jared, being favored of the Lord, and a man of mighty faith, did likewise. The third chapter, verses 21—25, Book of Ether, contain the following:

"And it came to pass that the Lord said unto the brother of Jared, Behold, thou shalt not suffer these things which ye have seen and heard, to go forth unto the world, until the time cometh that I shall glorify my name in the flesh: wherefore, ye shall treasure up the things which ye have seen and heard; and shew it to no man. And behold, when ye shall come unto me, ye shall write them and seal them up that no one can interpret them: for ye shall write them in a language that they cannot be read. And behold, these two stones will I give unto thee, and ye shall seal them up also, with the things which ye shall write. For behold, the language which ye shall write I have confounded, wherefore I will cause in my own due time that these stones shall magnify to the eyes of men these things which ye shall write. And when the Lord had said these words, He shewed unto the brother of Jared all the inhabitants of the earth which had been, and also all that would be: and he withheld them not from his sight unto the end of the earth."

"And the Lord commanded the brother of Jared to go down out of the mount from the presence of the Lord, and write the things which he had seen; and they were forbidden to come unto the children of men, until after that He should be lifted up upon the cross; and for this cause did king Mosiah keep them, that they should not come unto the world until after Christ should shew Himself unto His people. And after Christ truly had shewed Himself unto His people, He commanded that they should be made manifest. And now, after that, they have all dwindled in unbelief, and there is none, save it be the Lamanites, and they have rejected the Gospel of Christ; therefore I am commanded that I should hide them up again in the earth."—Ether, iv, 1—3.

Now, if the brother of Jared, of whom the Book of Mormon bears this record, and Votan, of whom the *Popol Vuh* and other historic ancient American writings, as we have seen, speak, are one and the same, then we can readily understand why he should write a book recording his genealogy and deeds, and giving an account of the wonderful things which Jesus, before He appeared in the flesh, had shown him, and why, also, he and his generations after him should guard the same and the *treasure* (the stones of interpretation) with such sacred care, for a period of perhaps not less than two thousand four hundred years.

Ether, who wrote his book about 600 B. C., being a great Prophet of God, was familiar with the writings and history of the brother of Jared, and it was doubtless through his record that it became understood that one of the descendants of Votan, and not Votan himself, had written the book; when the facts are, that they each wrote, but one many centuries previous to the other.

Moroni having again, about A. D. 420, hidden, by divine command, these books and the treasure in the earth, where they remained until brought forth by the great modern Prophet, Joseph Smith, it is clear that the bishop of Chiapas failed to destroy them.

Moses Thatcher.

CRIME AND EDUCATION.

THE zealous advocates of the increase of education among the masses, in their arguments in its favor as a preventive of crime, are apt to confound knowledge with wisdom; wisdom, if we mistake not, being the right use of knowledge. Many of the ideas these persons advance apply more directly to the moral powers of mankind than to their intellectuality; and the true reason why certain crimes are less frequent among some classes of society than among others, is to be attributed more to the fact that their moral training has not been neglected, than that they are learned in letters or in art.

There are certain crimes upon which the education of the common school, under the systems now most popular, has no apparent, and to the mind of the writer, can have no conceivable effect. For instance, crimes against chastity. No one who has any regard for the truth will argue that in the midst of the nations where grades of education exist, or, in other words, where the people are not all barbarous and totally uneducated, that adultery and its kindred infamies are especially and distinctively the sins of the uneducated. Rather, as it is generally admitted, these are the crimes of the rich, and consequently of the better educated. We here use the word education in its common acceptance, as the knowledge acquired at school, and in this sense desire it to be understood when hereafter used in this article.

Again, there are crimes wholly impossible to the utterly uneducated, forgery, peculation in office, falsification of accounts, and in a less degree, coining and counterfeiting. These evils will never be eradicated by simply filling the minds of men with book knowledge. The religious and moral nature of men must be trained, and the heart attuned to the love of truth and righteousness, before we may expect perceptible changes in society in this direction. On the other hand, the wider the spread of intellectuality and scholastic attainments, intermingled with religious skepticism and lax ideas regarding morality, the more prevalent will crimes of this class become, and the more difficult of detection; because, in the first place, of the artistic manner in which they will be conceived and carried out, and because of the apathetic and lukewarm moral sentiment of the community, which condones and partly encourages such wrongs, especially when committed by men of wealth, former social standing, or of influential connections.

What, then, are the crimes which it is asserted that education will lessen, if not obliterate? Crimes against property—theft, burglary, arson, etc.; and those of violence against the person—murder, manslaughter and other brutalities. Undoubtedly these crimes are more prevalent among the uneducated than the educated, but it is an open question whether primarily and originally education has anything to do with the matter. Is it not rather the state of society in which the uneducated, as a rule, are born and reared, and of which the absence of education is only one phase, which is responsible for this fact? These evils are manifested most largely amongst the poverty stricken; and it is their poverty that causes them to be uneducated, not their lack of education which causes them to be poor, only, as often happens, evils of this kind re-act and inter-act upon each other, the child of the poor is untaught, and, because he is untaught, when he grows up to manhood, he remains poor; he is at a disadvantage through the whole struggle of life.

Crimes against property can be traced to many causes which bear far more heavily upon the poor than upon the rich; and as the great bulk of the uneducated are found in the ranks of the poor the fault is improperly laid mainly to the want of education, while in truth that unfortunate fact should only bear an inconsiderable portion of the burden; we will notice a few of these causes.

Idleness. The poor man has to work, beg, or steal for a living; no such alternatives are presented to the rich. The lazy poor man, whether learned or untaught, has to beg, steal, or starve; as a rule he prefers to beg or steal, whilst the indolent rich man, be he fool or philosopher, can live without work or without stealing. Thus laziness, the fruitful mother of a thousand evils, is really the primary cause of many crimes which are popularly and thoughtlessly ascribed to ignorance, that is, to scholastic ignorance, for to ignorance, in its widest meaning, must be ascribed nine-tenths of the sins of mankind.

Poverty. The poor man is tempted by want, want of the necessities of life, of which the rich man experimentally knows nothing. The hungry and naked commit many crimes against property, which are simply the results of their condition. Let the positions of the classes be changed, the rich be made poor and the poor rich, we should then find that the previous scholastic or literary training of the former (if without natural moral stamina), would have little effect upon their actions when in want of bread. It would perhaps occasionally alter the description of the crime, the forger and his ilk would probably take the place of the burglar and the footpad.

Revenge. Many crimes against property, such as arson, willful destruction of property, maiming of animals, etc., are attributable to the feeling of revenge, or the antagonism of classes. This feeling is engendered and nurtured amongst the poor (and consequently the uneducated), because the wealthy have little or no cause, only in exceptional cases, for this feeling, and they know that their wrongs, if any, cannot be redressed in such ways; when the rich desire to exercise this feeling they call for the aid of the government, and accomplish their object by the power of the military; but when this is done it has little relation to the subject now under consideration, and arises more from political or social upheavals than from any individual infractions of the law. We have no doubt that more ignorant than educated men are charged with arson and the like, but if the crime be ascribed to lack of education it is not that education which the common school supplies. We are of the opinion that it more probably arises from too much of another kind of education, which confounds the rights of men, and teaches that one class of wrongs can be righted by the committal of other wrongs, and that those who esteem themselves oppressed are justified in injuring those whom they consider their oppressors. We maintain that individual crimes of this kind are not, as a rule, attributable to any influences or causes connected with the lack of education. We are not now considering the actions of men when aggregated as mobs, or as forces in rebellion against their governments—and even such require educated leaders. In such conditions of society, when the passions of men are violently inflamed, the education of the intellect has but little restraining force.

Squalor. Dirt, misery, degradation, and the other concomitants of poverty have much to do with these kinds of crime. The more men and women are huddled together like beasts in a corral, without any regard for the decencies of life, the less respect they will have for right as an abstract idea. They will be kept honest in action, by the fear of the rigors of the law; such honesty is, of course, only superficial, and breaks down under a very slight pressure, or whenever the chances of being detected are sensibly diminished. The low lodging houses and tenements of the large cities are hotbeds of vice, because they degrade man's moral nature, lessen his self respect, and teach a disregard for the proprieties and decencies of life, which is particularly injurious to the habits of the young, and render them peculiarly unfit to resist temptation. But this is the misfortune, not the fault of the poor; the wrong lies in the deficiencies and weaknesses of modern civilization.

Familiarity with crime. It is well said, "Familiarity breeds contempt," and in nothing more so than in regard to crime and its apparent consequences— the punishment which the law inflicts. Association with the habitual criminal, which is the lot of some of the very poor, has a manifest effect in the increase of crime. There is a remarkable characteristic apparent amongst many transgressors against the laws— the idea that they are too smart to be found out, or if found out, to be convicted. But few would deliberately commit offences if they imagined they would be punished. Criminals of this class are generally very hopeful individuals, and the frequent miscarriages of justice give them good reason for being so. As these characters are generally gathered from the lower strata of society, they naturally swell the number of criminals therein, and become another cause for the increase of crime in those classes, wrongfully attributed to lack of schooling.

The Inequality of the Laws, which in many countries bear more heavily upon the poor than on the well-to-do, may be placed among the causes that swell the ratio of uneducated criminals.

Severe Sentences for Minor Offences are a fruitful source of greater crimes. The period when the misery and degradation of the prison house is most keenly felt is during the first few months of confinement. During that time the punishment is most intense. After this, the feelings of strangeness and humiliation work off, the longing for friends and home wears away, and the prison becomes in part a home, poor though it be; at any rate, a place less to be dreaded; and the faces of officers and fellow prisoners grow familiar, and to an extent take the place of former friends and acquaintances. Habit is well said to be second nature, and as soon as a man becomes reconciled to prison life, the less worth will he be to society, and the less liklihood there is of his reformation when set free. Again, the longer he is kept confined the more unprepared will he be when at liberty to battle with the world or to "rustle for his grub," to use a prison phrase. Long confinement has made him enervated in body, and robbed him of manly ambition and independence. On the other hand, if he considers his sentence has been unjustly severe, and pronounced in the spirit of revenge, he broods over his supposed wrongs, and when his time is out he re-enters the world with the idea that he and society are at war, and that it is his business, if possible, to get the best of the conflict.

The rich man coming out of prison after a long sentence has no necessity to go to work, the poor man has but little inclination, or indeed bodily strength, and consequently, as a rule, falls back into evil ways. To this must be added the consideration of how difficult it is, in many communities, for a man once convicted of crime to obtain employment; he is a pariah, and an outcast, on whom his fellows frown, one who is almost compelled, for dear life's sake, through man's inhumanity to man, to resume the path of the transgressor. Thus again swelling the multitudes in the criminal classes, the majority of whom, for the reason above given, being the uneducated.

Bribery. There is yet another reason why often the poor are convicted, and the rich escape. It is that the latter are enabled to purchase a higher order of legal talent in their defence, and thus increase the chances of acquittal; while if this fail, it is notorious, that in many countries the rich can buy the officers of the law, if not by direct bribery, by the many little artifices known to those who dabble in such unclean waters. In fact, bribery has grown to be one of the fine arts of the nineteenth century.

These are some of the reasons why the uneducated, or the poorly educated, make so large a showing in our criminal calendar. The causes are not directly traceable to the want of the education of the common school, but to the entire environment of the classes in which the uneducated are most largely found. We have no fault to find with the training of the mind, but do not think it should stop there. To make men intellectual, and intellectual only, without the corresponding balances of religion and morality, will not decrease the criminal classes. The whole man must be educated, and the foundation laid in the love of truth and virtue. The wise man of old said, "The fear of the Lord is the beginning of wisdom," and we hold that his proposition is as true in the midst of the civilization of this age as it was in the earlier epochs of human history.

Geo. Reynolds.

To speak of a man as merely "good" has come to signify he is good for nothing.

LEAVES FROM THE TREE OF LIFE.

TENTH LEAF.

DEATH is the common heritage. It is a legacy to all the children, left by our first progenitor. It is the result of transgression, the penalty of violated law. The immortal pair who dwelt in Eden fell into mortality through sin. Immortality is the power of continued existence. But "all things are governed by law." Sin is law-breaking. To live for ever requires perpetual obedience to the laws of everlasting life. "That which is governed by law is preserved by law." By the same rule reversed, the reverse obtains. Therefore, that which is immortal and obeys not the laws of immortality, will become mortal. If obedience ensures preservation, disobedience involves destruction. Law reigns in the highest as well as in the lower spheres of being. Eternal life involves eternal compliance with the laws of existence.

All seeds produce their own kind. Mortal beings beget mortality. When the parents of our race became mortal through breaking a law of their immortal condition, they brought death to their offspring as well as to themselves. "In Adam all die." The curse of death smites the whole family. "It is appointed unto man once to die." No ingenuity he can exercise or precautions he can adopt will avert the impending doom. The decree has been proclaimed, "Thou shalt surely die," and it is irrevocable. The taint that came from the tree of death whose fruit was forbidden, descends to all generations, and every variety of form and feature, and color and stature, and tendency and peculiarity, have the one common characteristic, the certainty of death.

But is the dissolution of the body the end of existence? Not at all. We have seen that the part of man that comes from heaven lives on when that which came from the earth returns to the earth. Yet this is not sufficient. The query arises, Shall this body, made mortal through transgression, remain for ever under the penalty of the broken law, or is there some means of expiation for the sin and restoration from the doom, its consequence? Are all the associations formed in the flesh and pertaining to this mortal state, to perish with the decayed body and be scattered like the dust to which it is resolved? Are the fond relations of husband and wife, and parent and child to be dissolved forever? Is this exquisitely, "fearfully and wonderfully" formed mechanism, with the experiences of its temporal existence, to be obliterated and lose its identity in the material universe?

The answer comes down from the remotest ages, like sweet and sacred music whose tones swell and increase as the chorus is joined by the voices of the Prophets and Saints of each succeeding dispensation, until the grand harmony thrills every respondent soul. The burden of the song is in the words of the poetic Isaiah: "Thy dead men shall live; together with my dead body shall they arise! Awake and sing, ye that dwell in dust, for thy dew is as the dew of herbs and the earth shall cast out her dead!" And the ringing tones of Job the ancient are heard as a solo whose melody reaches unto heaven: "I know that my Redeemer liveth, and that He shall stand upon the earth in the latter day, and though after my skin worms destroy this body, yet in my flesh shall I see God!"

The faith of all people who have communed with God or have been inspired by the Holy Ghost, has been that they should be resurrected from the dead. They not only had the assurance of spirit life beyond the grave, but of the revivification of the material body. The signification of the word "resurrect" is "to stand up again." That which was laid down was to be raised up. The release of the immortal spirit from the mortal body would not answer to this. It was this mortal that was to put on immortality, this corruptible that was to put on incorruption.

To make this matter certain, Jesus, who expiated the primal sin, after being offered on the cross as the great sacrifice, gave up the ghost. His lifeless body was taken down, embalmed, and buried in a new tomb hewed out of the rock. It was guarded by Roman soldiers. On the third day from the interment that body came forth alive from the grave. The same Jesus who was crucified appeared again among His disciples, proved that the same body interred was brought forth again, by exhibiting the wounds made by the nails and the spear, by permitting them to touch Him, by eating and conversing with them, and by repeated visits. This was not a mere manifestation of the immortality of the soul, but a demonstration of the resurrection of the body. Yet that body was transformed. The corruptible blood was purged from the veins, and incorruptible spiritual fluid occupied its place. It was buried a natural body, it was resurrected a spiritual body. Here, then, was a pattern of that which is to come. This was the "first fruits of them that slept," a glorious sample of the great harvest of the summer of redemption.

Now the sacrifice of the Savior had as one of its chief objects the restoration of mankind to the condition lost by the fall. As in "Adam all die, so in Christ all are to be made alive." Death came to the race through one man's sin; life comes to the race through one man's atonement for that sin. The remedy is as broad as the disease, The plan is perfect. This is why Christ is called "The resurrection and the life." By virtue of His triumph over sin and His voluntary submission to death, which had no valid claim upon Him, being sinless, He obtained the keys of redemption for all the sleeping dust of the Adamic family. So He made no idle boast or mystic figure of speech when he declared, "The hour is coming in which all that are in their graves shall hear the voice of the Son of God, and shall come forth, they that have done good in the resurrection of the just, and they that have done evil in the resurrection of the unjust."

The raising of the dead, though universal, is not simultaneous. When Christ, who is our life, shall appear, He will first redeem those that are in Him. Having put on Christ and received of His spirit, they will come forth at His call to meet Him. They who have part in the first resurrection are those who have died in the Lord and are blessed and holy. Their bodies will be fashioned like unto His glorious body. "Having been planted in the likeness of His death they will be also in the likeness of His resurrection." That is, they will be quickened by the celestial glory and be placed in a condition to receive a fulness thereof, and inherit all things as joint heirs with Christ. The wicked dead remain unquickened for a thousand years. They reap the fruits of their evil seeds sown in lives of transgression. They drink the dregs of a bitter cup. Some are beaten with many stripes, others with but a few. Justice metes out to them their dues And when they come forth to stand up in their bodies, they will not be quickened by the celestial glory, but by that for which they are fitted by their respective conditions consequent upon their earthly acts, and they will occupy positions accordingly. But all will be redeemed in due season from the grave and stand the scrutiny of the All-Seeing Eye and the judgment of unswerving Justice, which will determine their eternal future.

In this age of general doubt, when human reason is exalted above divine testimony, and the voice of faith is drowned by the clamors of pretended science, the possibility and use of a resuscitation of the body are scouted and denied. But "all things are possible to them that believe," and the divinely illuminated mind can perceive not only the use, but the necessity of the resurrection. The being that was placed in Eden and endowed with power to wield dominion over all created things, was a living soul, a sentient spirit in an immortal body, a man fashioned in the image of God. He fell from that condition and paid the penalty of death. Christ's atonement, as we have seen, restores him to his original condition. But this he cannot have without his body again made immortal. By the workings of the grand scheme of human exaltation, he and his posterity, with the benefits of the lessons of experience, are restored to the immortality and pleasures of the primeval paradise, and placed on the path of eternal progress. And, mark this, a body framed out of the grosser elements is essential to the perfect happiness and power of the refined spiritual organism which possesses it as a tabernacle. The principle of affinities and of the attraction and communion of similars proclaims this truth. Spirit ministers to spirit. Things of a like nature cohere. The higher or spiritual element reaches upward to the loftiest things; the lower or fleshy element reaches downward, and the twain, inseparably combined and governed by the laws of right and truth, draw pleasure and delight from the heights and depths of the boundless universe and the ever extending sphere of eternal intelligence. A disembodied spirit is imperfect, and requires the clothing of its denser parts.

Without them, its affinities would lie in but one direction, and its joy and progress would be limited. The family condition too is formed in the embodied state. Death separates the husband and wife, the parents and children. The resurrection, in its highest conditions, reunites them and restores all that was lost in the grave. Who can picture the bliss, the glory, the power, the might, the dominion and majesty that shall grow out of the redemption from the dead of the righteous man and his household, dwelling in perfect harmony and peace with all the powers of their being, spiritual and physical, purified, quickened, intensified and enlarged to a fulness, with all eternity before them for the exercise thereof in accordance with the designs of the Great Creator? It is beyond the skill of man to depict it, and no mortal mind can comprehend it without special divine illumination.

And who shall define the impossible, or draw the bounds of the powers of the Creator? The secret of ordinary life is hidden from the scrutiny of the most profound scientist. He knows not the mystery of the vital principle that quickens even the lowest form of animated nature. His own powers of mind and motion are incomprehensible to him. Their origin and cause are beyond his ken, and he cannot solve the problem any better than the ignorant Hottentot or the untutored Indian. The reproduction of plants from their seeds, the evolving of life out of the midst of their death, is a wonder unexplained. And shall we say that it is impossible for the Power that regulates the universe to reanimate a defunct body? It must be remembered that nothing in nature is annihilated. No particle of matter is destroyed by any process. What is called death is but a change of form. All matter is not visible to the human eye. A body may exist, but so transformed as to be imperceptible to the natural vision. The forces that regulate the universe are occult, and though some of the laws that govern them are known, there are others that have not been discovered, and it is the height of presumption for those who have obtained a smattering of information concerning these things—and who has obtained more?—to declare that impossible which they know nothing of, or to limit the power of that creative or quickening energy, whose nature, capabilities and qualities they cannot comprehend in the smallest degree.

If one dead body has been raised to life, unnumbered millions may also be revived. That one we have in the person of Jesus of Nazareth, and He is the forerunner of all the race. Let the sons and daughters of men rejoice and give thanks to Him who has wrought out this great redemption. Death is conquered. The grave has no terrors. Life and immortality are brought to light. Eternity with all its prospects and capabilities is opened to the view. And through the power of the resurrection vested in Christ Jesus, the whole globe shall deliver up its dead, and the great progenitor of our race, Adam, the "Ancient of Days," shall stand forth at the head of his posterity all quickened and animated by the spirit of life; and while Jesus the Son is hailed as the mighty Redeemer, God the Eternal Father shall be honored and worshiped for ever as the author of our being, from whom springs all life, light, power and glory throughout the vast domains of universal space!

C. W. Penrose.

TRAVELS IN ITALY.

X.
THE VATICAN AND CATACOMBS.

WE have at home in our cabinet of curiosities, collected abroad, a small shrivelled orange; the incident which makes it worthy of preservation, will introduce the reader to the Pope's garden, in one of the open courts of the Vatican palace.

While going from St. Peter's to the palace, we came suddenly through a spacious hall to a door opening upon a most beautiful grove of orange and olive trees. The walks about the edge of this lovely garden were scrupulously kept. The custodian occupied a small lodge in one corner, and was standing in the doorway as we passed. We were strongly tempted to secure some of the delicious fruit that hung in golden balls about our heads, and put forth our hands as if intending to pluck some of it. The custodian sprang forward and, with hands uplifted, said several *ave marias*, looked most woefully offended, and finally knelt and prayed for the forgiveness of the poor souls that had committed the sacrilege of coveting an orange from the garden of his holiness the Pope. We put our hands into our pockets and passed on into the sculpture galleries, where we remained several hours. On returning through the garden, we were astonished when the piously offended custodian beckoned us into his lodge, and handed us several of the fine fresh oranges we had so wickedly desired shortly before. He had observed that when we left him we placed our hands in our pockets, and this was too significant even for the most devoted of the Pope's household. He waived all scruples, prepared to make confession, and get absolution on the morrow, and joyfully accepted the small silver pieces we placed in his hand. This is characteristic of the devotees of Catholicism who act as guides, police, custodians of churches, art galleries or public gardens—in a word, of all that part of the community which receives a fee, and it is a large part; they will, in the same moment, beseech God to forgive the impiety of breaking any regulation, and, for a fee, proceed to break it.

In the last number, we indicated the extent of the galleries devoted to art in this great art palace of the world. How shall we portray their beauty? The *Loggie* and *Stanze* of Raphael are chief among them. The former contains the wonderful frescoes painted by the great master, and divided into thirteen sections; together they are known as "Raphael's Bible." The first twelve represent upwards of fifty scenes from the Old Testament, with a great many fauciful portraits of the great characters of Scriptural celebrity from Adam, Noah and Abraham, down. The thirteenth section of this great artistic achievement represents scenes in the life of Christ. The *Stanze* are four saloons, containing remarkable ceiling decorations and frescoes on the walls, of great interest and beauty. The ceiling paintings of one room represent Theology, Poetry, Philosophy and Justice, while the pictures on the walls below are allegories, in which many varied characters are introduced, from the saints ministering around the Lord, to Dante, Savonarola and Boccaccio.

The museum of statues includes upwards of a dozen galleries, commencing with a corridor twenty-five hundred feet in length, in which are several thousand heathen and early Christian inscriptions, sarcophagi and small statues.

The collection of antiquities, particularly of ancient Grecian sculpture, of the Vatican, is the finest in the world. In each of the galleries, which contain many departments, some great and surprising statue, bust or inscription will be met to elicit the warmest praise, and call forth sincere admiration. In the first hall entered, there is a colossal group called The Nile. It consists of an enormous marble figure, lying recumbent, and surrounded by sixteen playing children, emblematic of the sixteen yards which the river rises; at the back and sides of the statue, a humorous representation of a battle between the pigmies and the crocodiles and hippopotami is seen. In the same room is a fine statue of Demosthenes.

In the vestibule of the Belvedere, the most renowned and interesting of all the saloons, is the celebrated Torso of Hercules, executed, according to the inscription, by Apollonius of Athens, in the first century B. C.; it was found in the sixteenth century near the theatre of Pompey. Passing through the vestibule, we enter the Court of the Belvedere, an octagonal room, surrounded with arcades, which are separated by four apartments,

in which several of the most important works of the collection are placed. The cabinet or department of Canova contains the statue of Perseus and several others by that artist. In the third apartment, is the celebrated group that has no equal in marble grouping in the world: Laocoon with his two sons entwined by the snakes. This statue was executed by sculptors of ancient Rhodes, and once was placed, according to the historian Pliny, in the palace of the Emperor Titus, who took Jerusalem. It was discovered in the year 1506, and was termed by Michael Angelo, a marvel of art. The work is admirably preserved. "In the delicacy of workmanship, the dramatic suspense of the moment, and the profoundly expressive attitudes of the heads, especially that of the father, it is the grandest representative of the Rhodian school of art." The fourth apartment of the saloon contains the Apollo Belvedere, without exception the most universally admired of ancient sculptures. It was found near the gates of Antium, at the end of the fifteenth century. It is a statue of Carrara marble, and represents the god in the act of striking terror into the Celts, who had dared to attack his sanctuary of Delphi.

The following stanzas from Byron's Childe Harold's Pilgrimage, better describe "The Laocoon and Apollo" than any other words written in the English:

Or, turning to the Vatican, go see
Laocoon's torture dignifying pain—
A father's love and mortal's agony
With an immortal's patience blending—vain
The struggle; vain against the coiling strain
And gripe, and deepening of the dragon's grasp,
Rivets the living links—the enormous asp
Enforces pang on pang, and stifles gasp on
    gasp.

Or, view the Lord of the unerring bow,
The God of life, and poesy, and light—
The sun in human limbs array'd, and brow
All radiant from his triumph in the fight;
The shaft hath just been shot—the arrow bright
With an immortal's vengeance; in his eye
And nostril beautiful disdain, and might,
And majesty, flash their full lightnings by,
Developing in that one glance the Deity.

But in his delicate form—a dream of love,
Shaped by some solitary nymph, whose breast
Long'd for a deathless lover from above,
And madden'd in that vision—are exprest
All that ideal beauty ever bless'd
The mind within its most unearthly mood,
When each conception was a heavenly guest—
A ray of immortality—and stood
Starlike, around, until they gather'd to a god!

And if it be Pometheus stole from heaven
The fire which we endure, it was repaid
By him to whom the energy was given
Which this poetic marble hath array'd
With an eternal glory, which, if made
By human hands, is not of human thought;
And Time himself hath hallowed it, nor laid
One ringlet in the dust—nor hath it caught
A tinge of years, but breathes the flame with
   which 'twas wrought.

The tapestry of Raphael is found in a room leading from the museum of sculpture. Each piece is from designs of the great master, derived from the history of the New Testament. They are among the most admirable of his works. Seven of the original tapestries were bought by Charles I of England, and are exhibited in the South Kensington Museum, London. Those remaining in the Vatican, each cost about four thousand dollars. They are skillfully hand-wrought works of the most delicate character, wool, silk and threads of gold being employed in their manufacture. The finer tints of the coloring are much faded. These tapestries were designed to occupy the lower walls of the Sixtine Chapel, but were superseded by the wonderful paintings of Michael Angelo.

The remaining art galleries of the Vatican, including the Egyptian Museum, the Etruscan Antiquities, the Great Picture Gallery, the Library, which contains upwards of twenty-five thousand valuable manuscripts and is in charge of a cardinal, and the Studio of Mosaics, must all be passed over, the limits of space not permitting more than mention of them. Days and weeks might be profitably employed in visiting the extensive collections of marble, canvas and endless works of art which throng the corridors and enliven the innumerable apartments of the Vatican, which is truly the greatest art gallery in the world.

The Catacombs afford to Christians a means of bridging the chasm that seems, from the modern aspect of the city, to separate Ancient and early Christian Rome. They were the burying places of the early Christians, and are located beyond the walls of the ancient city. A Roman law forbade the burying of the dead, or even the deposit of their ashes, within the city limits, hence the Columbaria, where the urns are placed, and the Catacombs, where interments were made, are both without the gates of Rome. A desire to inter the dead, instead of cremating them, gave rise to the excavation of these subterraneous passages, which are thirty feet under ground. They are about three feet wide, and on either side are apertures large enough to receive a human body; these are located one above another, reaching to the top of the passage, which may be ten feet. The Catacombs were used almost exclusively for Christian burial, the pagans universally believing in and practising cremation.

A popular fallacy that the Catacombs were secret burying places, to which the Christians resorted to avoid the pagan law of cremation, has long been exploded. The interments were conducted publicly, and the burying places were under the supervision of inspectors. The labyrinth of aisles is close and oppressive, the utmost darkness prevails, relieved only by a small wax taper which each visitor carries. The sensation is singular and awful as one goes tramping through these narrow ways which separate the dead. The Catacombs of Calixtus are the most extensive and interesting. On the twenty-second day of November, St. Cecilia's day, mass is said there, and they are illuminated. One can hardly imagine anything more wierd than the sight thus produced; but there is nothing held in greater reverence by the priests and Catholic communities than these resting places of the early Christians. *De Vallibus.*

Employment makes people happy.

CHRONICLES OF UTAH.

VI.

By July 24th, 1851, although only four years since the advent of the Pioneers, Great Salt Lake City had assumed quite a business aspect; and the various settlements throughout the Territory were in a flourishing condition. The celebration of the twenty-fourth of July was observed with the usual ceremonies, the day being one of unusual loveliness and splendor. The Nauvoo Brass Band, in their mammoth carriage, delighted the citizens with their sublime strains of martial and cheering music; accompanied by the roaring of cannon, the people thronging the streets as they approached the Bowery, on the Temple ground, where the companies were organized for the procession. Bands of music led the van. The Nauvoo Brass Band first in order, then a military band, each with appropriate banners; then the Pioneers, with a banner representing the memorable day of crossing the Platte, inscribed with motto, "Blessings Follow Sacrifice," each Pioneer bearing an emblem of his calling, such as was necessary in making a new settlement; then followed the Regents of the University, each carrying a book; flag and motto, inscribed thereon, "All Truth;" next came the aged fathers, with flag and motto, "Heroes of '76;" then twenty-four boys, uniformed, white pants and straw colored roundabouts, straw hats and blue sashes, banner, "Hope of Israel;" then twenty-four mothers in Israel, banner, motto, "Our Children are our Glory;" twenty-four young girls dressed in white, pink scarfs, with banner, motto, "Virtue dwells in Zion;" twenty-four young men, black coats, white pants and red sash, banner with inscription, "Lion of the Lord;" twenty-four young ladies, dressed in white, with wreaths of roses on their heads, blue scarfs, and bearing a banner, "Hail to our Chieftain;" next, the national flag, the Stars and Stripes of the United States; then followed Brigham Young, H. C. Kimball, W. Richards, John Smith, Patriarch; Dr. J. M. Bernhisel, Mr. Harris, Secretary of the Territory; Judge Brandenburg, Judge Z. Snow, Mr. Race, Sub-Indian Agent; then twenty-four Bishops, dressed in uniform, each bearing a flag with some appropriate device. This party was escorted to the Bowery, where it was were received with cheering and the discharge of cannon. After the large audience was called to order, there was singing and prayer; Gen. D. H. Wells then rose and delivered an oration appropriate to the occasion. Music, singing, speeches and toasts followed in order; after which, the procession reformed, and escorted the party to the Governor's house, where a sumptuous dinner was prepared for the officers of the Territory and other invited friends. The latter part of the day was passed in great freedom and enjoyment. The report of the Committee of Arrangements, states that "the order and decorum which prevailed in such a crowded audience, showed that the Spirit of God pervaded the breasts of all. Every countenance was graced with a smile, and the people returned to their respective homes, thanking the Giver of all Good that they were privileged to witness such happy scenes, and to worship Him under their own vine and fig tree, and none to make them afraid." The Committee of Arrangements were D. H. Wells, J. M. Grant, Seth M. Blair, Jeter Clinton, H. S. Eldredge, A. H. Raleigh, L. W. Hardy, S. W. Richards and Joseph Cain.

August 19. The *Deseret News* issued the thirty-ninth number, closing the first volume of that paper; the editor informed his patrons that "should the *News* be continued, it would be on an enlarged sheet of twice the size, and more than twice the amount of reading matter." Accordingly, on November 15, 1851, No. 1 of Vol. II appeared, Willard Richards, editor and proprietor, as before. We are told, among other things, that "the affairs of Utah were in a flourishing condition." "The companies prepared in October to settle at Salt Creek and Millard County, Fillmore City, were at their destination, and engaged in their improvements." A small company had gone twenty miles north of Weber, commenced a fort, and were preparing for farming and lumbering. The public works of Great Salt Lake City were prospering; the railway to the stone quarries on the east of the city, for bringing down rock to the Temple Block was nearly completed; public barns as well as private buildings had been enclosed and finished. Of news from Europe, it is stated that the *Etoile du Deseret* (The Star of Deseret), had been published at Paris, by Elder John Taylor, and more than four thousand five hundred persons had been baptized in England by our Elders, during the first six months of 1851.

From manuscripts, formerly in the possession of the late President Willard Richards, the following extracts from a letter to the Earl of Derby, dated December 9, 1839, are taken:

"To the Rt. Honorable Lord Derby:

SIR:—We, the undersigned, your petitioners, representatives of the Church of "Latter-day Saints," in Preston and vicinity, beg leave to represent to your lordship, that for a considerable time previous to the last quarter, said Church met regularly for religious worship, on the Sabbath, in the building called *The Cock Pit*, for which we paid a stipulated sum, according to previous contract with the occupants of the same; but during the last quarter we have been deprived of the use of said building, from some cause, or causes to us unknown; for, although it was reported that the "Cock Pit" had changed owners, and was to be devoted to other purposes, yet, as it remains unoccupied, we are inclined to believe the report delusive, and consequently suppose your lordship still to be the sole proprietor of the same; and as we have little covering for our religious work at Preston but the blue arch of heaven, and no other convenient place offers to our view, we beg humbly to petition that your lordship will be graciously pleased to grant us the free use of said "Cock Pit" for our religious worship on the Sabbath, for the time being, or while we need it, and your lordship does not require it for other purposes; or if it be more congenial to your lordship's feelings, that your lordship will cause the same to be let to your petitioners for the above purpose, for a stipulated sum, such as your petitioners may be able to meet with their limited means, &c:"

The petition was signed by Willard Richards, Joseph Fielding and William Clayton, as presiding Elders of said Church of Latter-day Saints, and is dated, "Preston, Dec. 9th, 1839, from the new house opposite No. 3 Meadow Street." The letter was intrusted to the care of Peter Melling, as delegate, and a statement of the principles of the Gospel as received by us as a people, was forwarded for the information of the Earl of Derby. The mention of the "Cock Pit" of Preston, will bring to the memory of thousands the doings of the Elders in the early history of the British Mission. It appears that gross misrepresentations had been made respecting our religious faith and practices, which had prejudiced the public mind, and led to the expulsion of our people from the "Cock Pit," in which thousands had heard the words of life and salvation. It was to rectify these evils that the above petition had been prepared.

During this important year, the people in the valleys labored under great difficulties in obtaining supplies of nails and other iron articles; settlements were forming on every hand, buildings being erected; for this reason, a company was sent to Iron County to try to make iron; great efforts were also made in paper making and other manufactures. The responsible duties of the Governor of the Territory called forth all the energies of President Brigham Young; in the midst of these labors, Judges Brandenburg and Brocchus, Secretary Harris and Captain Day, Indian sub-agent, left for the States in September. On the twenty-first of October, the Governor, however, proceeded to the south, accompanied by Heber C. Kimball and Geo. A. Smith, the Board of Commissioners for locating the seat of Government for Utah; his Honor, Judge Snow, Gen. D. H. Wells, Major Race, sub-Indian agent, and several other distinguished citizens left Great Salt Lake City for Parowan Valley; they passed through Utah and Juab Counties by the lower ford of the Sevier and across Lake Valley, and reached Chalk Creek, in Parowan Valley, October 28th. On the twenty-ninth, the site for the seat of Government was determined about a mile east of the ford; the city was named Fillmore, and the county, Millard; a view of this site was painted by Majors, with the liberty pole and surrounding country; this lovely work of art is now in the Deseret Museum. The Governor and company returned by way of Sanpete Valley, where Judge Snow organized the Second Judicial District at Manti, in the county of Sanpete.

The work of colonization went on rapidly, improvements were made in every settlement, schoolhouses being among the first public buildings. The laws of health were publicly explained; lectures on astronomy and the sciences generally were delivered; the parent school gave instructions to qualify teachers for the territorial schools; native industries were encouraged; saleratus and other salts found here were largely used for bread making, soap manufacture, etc., etc.; cut nails were made from wagon tires and scrap iron to, supply present wants; iron making was started by forming a company in Iron County.

On the fifth of December, the Old Bowery was unroofed, and the material used for the Tabernacle, which was being finished. Many pleasing associations are connected with the Bowery, which was in constant use for public and private meetings, concerts, dramatic entertainments, readings, lectures, etc.

Much had been done during the year 1851 to improve the city and Territory; Great Salt Lake City had been incorporated; charters had been granted to Ogden, Provo, Manti and Parowan; Fillmore City had been located as the seat of Government and the Capital of Utah; Millard, Box Elder and Carson Counties had been settled; a capacious Tabernacle, one hundred and twenty-six by sixty-four feet, capable of seating three thousand people, had been erected and nearly completed; grain mills and saw mills were made in all the counties of Utah; minerals were discovered and utilized.

There was constant work for everyone to do; the people were few and the labors were most arduous to perform; mechanics and laborers all had their hands full; our professional men, Jesse W. Fox and others, in surveying; Professor Orson Pratt, and assistants, engaged in making observations and calculations on latitude, altitude, variation, etc., etc., for the different cities and settlements. To mention the names of all who were prominent in building up Zion would be impossible in a limited notice; when the history of our cities shall be written, it is to be hoped that justice will be done by the youth of Israel to the memory of their fathers.

Beta.

"ANTI-JEWS" IN GERMANY.

GERMANY is disturbed by an anti-Semitic movement, which has even entered the universities. Grave professors and theoretic students are alike excited, either for or against the movement to pull down the Jews. The explanation of this anti-Jewish excitement is simply this:

The Jews have succeeded, by their shrewdness and executive ability, in obtaining control of the money and the press of Germany. By means of these powerful levers they are raising themselves slowly and surely to commanding positions in commerce, law and politics. Their prosperity has attracted to Germany thousands of Jews anxious to elevate themselves. As is natural, the Germans are exasperated at the fact that they, after having won glorious victories on the battle-fields of France and Austria, should be beaten in the more material fields of commerce and politics.

A gentleman, residing in Berlin, sends to an Albany journal the following description of an "anti-Semitic" scene in the university of that city:

Professor ——, a "baptized Jew," was lecturing upon the history of philosophy, before a large audience of students. He had finished the Egyptians and had come to the Greeks.

"The Greeks, gentlemen, were indeed philosophers, genuine philosophers, with all the excellencies and defects of the philosophical •mind. Yes, gentlemen, they were weak enough even to hate the Jews."

Hissing, howls, applause—an absolute pandemonium of noise—greeted this foolhardy digression.

Fortunately the hour was at an end, and the agitators had to delay any further uproar until the following lecture.

A half-hour before the beginning of the lecture, the auditorium, the second largest in the university, was filled to overflowing with students.

The professor, foreseeing that an attempt to reach his rostrum might be attended with considerable difficulty, was early in his place, and by the time he rose to speak, the room and all its approaches were crammed with men, who were bent on mischief.

Precisely at the end of the academic "quarter"—a German professor never begins till a quarter of an hour after the advertised time—Professor —— arose, sipped a glass of water (not beer), and began: "Meine herr'n, Socrates war der erste" (Socrates was the first)—he had finished! What might have been the end of this promising proposition the world will probably never know.

"Socrates!" was echoed from a dozen parts of the room. "Socrates wasn't a Jew." "Give us something about the Jews." "Take it back! Take it back!" "Retract!" "Dare you say it again?" [Referring to the remark of the previous lecture]. "Lie! lie! lie! You vulgar liar!"

And, will you believe it, the professor so far forgot himself and the dignity of his position as to shout out in return, "I am no Jew!" "Baptized Jew!" came back to him as from a pack of maniacs. "Leopard can't change his spots!"

The man tried again and again to get a hearing, but in vain. The students would listen to nothing. In parts of the room you could see at times some arch conspirator standing on a desk and haranguing neighbors or reading some incendiary article from a newspaper.

Finally, after affairs had quieted down somewhat through the sheer weariness of the audience—audience is, by the way, a fair word here—the professor made himself heard, but only to remark, in a mild tone—

"Gentlemen, it seems somewhat unquiet here, and the room a little too small; would we not do well to go into the barracks?"—a large building which is used by the professors in their largely attended "popular lectures."

Instantly there was a stampede for the barracks. It was filled at once, and the students were again in readiness to continue matters.

Not so, however, their worthy teacher. He simply made the best of the opportunity to take French leave, and the students who had assembled this second time only to hear from the Dean of the Philosophical Faculty that "Professor —— would not lecture to-night."

"We will have him!" "We will have him!" "Send him to us or we will go and take him!" "Send us the cursed Jew!" was their answer.

They were furious at being cheated of their prey, and proposed to spend the remaining portion of the time by venting their anger through speeches and resolutions. At this crisis, however, the old janitor appeared on the scene, and in one small speech effected what the accomplished professor and venerable dean were powerless to bring about.

In a shrill, piping voice, and with a nasal twang of which only a born Berliner is capable, he merely remarked—

"Meine Herrn: In precisely two minutes the gas will be turned off."—*Youth's Companion*.

MONOTONIES OF LIFE.

"Let the great world spin forever, ·
Down the ringing grooves of change."
Tennyson.

IN a former article under this caption, it was the writer's main endeavor to depict examples of monotony as it is presented to the sight. The audible world is quite as prolific of illustration, and perhaps even more so than the visible. Who has not felt or noticed the effect upon the senses, of a protracted duration or continual recurrence of sound? Among the best of soporifics is the ripple of a stream, the patter of the rain, or the voice of a tiresome preacher. They may not be equally agreeable in operation, but they are all wonderfully effective in producing sleep.

No public meeting is the proper place to indulge in slumber, and I esteem not at all highly the individual who makes a practice of attending church for such purposes. He would much better remain at home, where his nasal soliloquies would not compete with the voice of the minister, and his example be less contagious to others of somnolent propensities; nevertheless, I verily believe there are times when the preacher is more to be censured than the listener, and when the act of falling asleep during a sermon, should excite less blame than commiseration. Any sound, unduly prolonged, especially when no respect is paid to variety of tone or expression, we soon weary of, and a discourse, oration, or dialogue, though teeming with instruction, loses much of its force, and falls short of its purpose, when its medium is a dry and tedious delivery. The principle herein—to digress for a moment—holds also with regard to a speaker's appearance in public. He who wishes to hold influence over the masses, must not appear too frequently before them. No matter how imposing his appearance, splendid his diction, or elegant his address, or how powerful and eloquent a reasoner he may be: if he is seen or heard too often, interest in him will abate correspondingly, appreciation of his ability will vanish, and he will soon be

10

devoid of the influence he once swayed over the mind and heart of the multitude. He who aims to be an agreeable converser, must not keep his tongue perpetually going. He must take his turn as a listener, giving others an occasional chance to speak, or he will be considered as a bore, and admiration for his talents will be turned into disgust for his egotism. The very secret of power often lies in the mastery over the tongue: "Even the fool, when he holdeth his peace, is counted wise; and he that shutteth his lips, is esteemed a man of understanding."

A mere numbskull, by saying nothing, has more than once impressed the awe-stricken circle around him with the idea that he was a profound thinker; when the fact was that he said nothing, for the simple reason that he had nothing to say. Silence was his forte, and he had sense enough to know it and act accordingly. Many a one, equally ignorant, has made himself ridiculous by neglecting to do likewise. To obtain an illustration of the influence of silence, one has but to go into an evening company. Not a gossip gathering, where the longest tongue is the test of excellence; not where Fashion and Frivolity are the presiding deities, where one might spend the period of his natural life without hearing a single sentiment worth remembering; but an intelligent company, where literature, art, science, politics and religion are occasional themes of conversation. Go there, and listen to the babbler, who "knows it all;" who has something to say upon every subject, and in matters up for discussion assumes the position of oracle to the rest. Observe then, the individual, if such there be, who keeps a silent tongue until his opinion is solicited, then submits his views modestly, plainly, in few words but with a quiet telling emphasis on all. You will not be long in deciding which is the more impressive, and wields most influence. "Speech is silver, but silence is gold."

A common illustration of the effect of monotony, will be noticed in the neighborhood of a person addicted to scolding; in the schoolroom, place of business, or the home circle. A want of influence is immediately apparent. The teacher who is eternally railing at his pupils, inspires nothing but contempt, unless it be amusement, which under the circumstances, is about the same thing. The noisier he is, the noisier his school will be; and so it is with the head of a family, the manager of a theatre, the overseer of an establishment, or any one holding authority over others. The one who scolds will be scolded in return, just as surely as like produces like, and according to the scriptural declaration that whatsoever is meted out by one shall be meted unto him in return.

> "Speak gently; it is better far,
> To rule by love than fear."

Not only is it better, but ninety-nine cases in a hundred, it is far easier to rule by kindness than to enforce obedience by harshness and cruelty. Human nature instinctively rebels against unkind treatment, and the finest and noblest natures are the ones which feel, if they do not resent it the quickest. I never could comprehend why so many believe in and advocate harsh language as a necessity. The rude drover will take his oath that his cattle mind him better when he storms and shouts invectives at them; the profane ruffian says it does him good to free his mind by a volley of oaths, and the shrewish housekeeper solemnly affirms that she must scold and threaten in order to be properly understood and obeyed. That she becomes properly understood is very likely; the language which escapes unstudied from a person's lips, is generally a fair index to the mind where it originated, as the character of the natural fruit is a criterion of the tree which produced it; but that she is more readily obeyed, than she would be if she adopted a milder method, is a delusion as false as it is foolish. There is just as much reason in the declaration of the cattle drover or the ruffian, that his word has more influence or his mind is benefited by coarseness and profanity, as in the vain imagination that angry speech,

complaining or faultfinding in the household, will better secure its end, than could be effected by an opposite course. Because a person has adopted scolding as a habit, and taught others to expect it whenever he comes within hearing, and because anything of a gentler nature would pass unheeded, or only awaken a momentary surprise in the listener, not used to hearing or obeying anything of so soft a character from such a source; no argument is furnished to support the erroneous doctrine that scolding is a necessity. Habit, and habit only, is amenable in such a case. The secret of good government is a kind heart, a firm will and few words.

A monotony of any kind we soon learn to disregard and treat with indifference, and if forced upon us, we sicken speedily and sigh after a change. Let the reader imagine himself the inmate of a dungeon cell, subsisting upon bread and water, with little or nothing to enliven the dull, tedious hours, that drag like a lengthening chain, coil after coil, binding him day by day closer to despair and wretchedness; his sight bounded by the four walls of his prison, his hearing oppressed by the continuous clank of chains or the harsh grating of his rusty door, and his taste cloyed by the stale and scanty provender doled out from day to day, which he must either swallow loathingly and mechanically, or reject and suffer from the pangs of hunger. Would not such a person be apt to appreciate a change of life and diet? Take an opposite example. The pampered child of wealth, born and reared in a palace, where every wish is gratified before expressed, every word the law to a score of surrounding menials, and whose only care is to seek after pleasure and pursue it till satiety ensues; whose life is an empty, glittering dream, whose mind is a playground for every idle impulse, and who is constantly miserable because his time and talents are unoccupied, and he has everything that heart can desire excepting the desire to enjoy it. Would not such a one appreciate variety, even at the sacrifice of wealth and position?

Yet there are persons who consider a

desire for change indicative of a fickle and unreliable disposition. From one point such a view is based upon reason, and supported by numerous illustrations; but is it not the perversion of legitimate taste, and the wanton abuse of its privileges, that furnish such a prospect? A propensity for changing opinions, principles, situations or possessions, without good reason therefor, should always be deprecated. The political turncoat, whose policy is self interest; the hypocrite who changes his countenance as the chameleon changes its hue; the apostate, who renounces his faith as often as he loses his temper; the volatile tradesman who flits from one business to another; the weak headed controversialist, who argues on all sides of a question within twenty-four hours and has no settled opinion upon any; these are examples of changeability which none should desire to shield from the contempt they ought universally to excite; and as in the case of the ancient Greek burgher, who wanted Aristides banished because he was tired of hearing him called "the Just," are not entitled to respectful consideration in the light of the proverb: "Variety is the spice of life."

To flit through life like a butterfly among flowers; forming attachments in a moment, and breaking them in the next; half accomplishing one thing and deserting it for another; avowing friendship while the sun shines, to prove false when the storm lowers; imagining life was made for pleasure and having no nobler aim than pleasure; these indeed would indicate fickleness and unreliability, but not to glean knowledge from every righteous source, utilize it in every wise direction; acquire true and lasting friendships, and enjoy the wholesome beauties of variety which the hand of God has scattered around in endless and magnificent profusion. A desire for change is perfectly legitimate, and should be indulged when springing from a proper motive. There is a time for labor and a time for rest; a time for waking and a time for sleeping; a time for gayety and a time for reflection, and each is rendered doubly enjoyable by judicious

and appropriate alternation. The desire for change is not only legitimate, but absolutely necessary. Without it there could be no advancement. It should be encouraged when it prompts us to progress, to lay aside false notions, and embrace new ideas whose authenticity has been established; but it should be restrained when it would induce us to forsake the tried and proven simply because it is old, and adopt the untried and novel, simply because it is new.

The world is peopled in variety. The rich are here to feed the poor, the strong to protect the weak, the wise to teach the foolish, the righteous to reclaim the wicked. These are duties expected of them, for the performance of which they will be held rigidly accountable. Thus is man tested and proven. It is essential for the opposing principles of good and evil to exist, that he may intelligently survey them and choose which he will serve. For it is only by studying the nature of the one that he can form a due estimate of the other. The world is full of variety, and God has designed it for the fulfillment of his purposes. And will there be no variety in heaven? Are its unchangeable laws incompatible with sensate diversities? Is it there eternal progress and variety, or endless stagnation and monotony? Our sectarian friends would fain convert us to the latter belief, but the light of revelation dispels such a delusion. Celestial beings are not subject to retrgression, and by what other name could such a change be called? Those who secure eternal life, divested of fault and developed in perfection, will not only retain the essential traits and features which distinguish them here, but united in heavenly harmony will engage in innumerable congenial pursuits, for which they are severally fitted and designed.

If variety on earth be legitimate, in heaven it will be indispensable; if here it be conducive to comfort, it will there be essential to happiness. Man's talents that are developed in time, will all be employed in eternity, and the wisdom he acquires on earth, will rise with him in the resurrection.   *O. F. Whitney.*

MOUNT EYRIE.

MANY hundreds of tourists go abroad annually from the Eastern and Middle States, to see the mountain scenes of Switzerland and the Tyrol. They are ignorant of the grandeur and beauty of the mountain regions of our own country. They know nothing of the towering peaks and deep ravines, the green vales and shimmering lakes, which abound in the Rocky range of the Great West. Not only are people of the East unacquainted with the treasures of natural scenery with which we, in the Great Salt Lake Basin, are surrounded, but many of our own residents, reposing in the towns and cities of the large valleys, are in equal oblivion of the pleasure and delight that would greet them, on winding through the numerous cañons and climbing to the mountain tops, which invite their inspection on every hand.

Every mountain gap or open cañon possesses charms which, once discovered, remain green in the memory forever. Towering rocks in grotesque shapes, vegetation of every shade and hue, evergreen and fern, rippling streams and roaring torrents, waterfalls and deep moss-bound pools, contribute to the enchantment of the visitor. An occasional deer or mountain lion, flocks of grouse, chirping squirrels, and shoals of mountain trout afford employment for gun and fishing rod; wild strawberries, grapes and clusters of elderberries tempt the fruit-gatherer; while wild roses, blue-bells, larkspurs, violets and primroses blossom in freshness on the hillsides, and fill the air with their fragrance.

The attractions of the Cottonwood cañons are most alluring to Salt Lake residents. The massive walls of granite, rising to stupendous heights on either side of the road, present varied forms and are grim and terrible in their silent grandeur. The rapids of the "Stairs," a few miles up Big Cottonwood, excite and bewilder the traveler, the water tumbling in wild confusion over the projecting rocks, foaming and roaring on its course to the broad fields in the valley below. The old sawmills, with overshot water wheels and piles of slabs, lumber and refuse lying around them, are picturesque enough for the painter's eye, and enliven the dead silence of the road with a hum and buzz, that refresh and please the traveler, as he peers from the carriage doors upon the field of logs, scattered around and blocking up his way.

When the valley of Silver Lake, at the head of the cañon, is reached, the very climax of beauty in mountain scenery is attained. Interlaken is not more enchanting. The timber covered hills around are green and fragrant; the balsam odors from the pine groves, lading the cool, light air with healing sweets that invigorate and strengthen the system as nothing else can do. Great blocks of granite are strewn about the low, rolling hills which encompass the beautiful lake and lovely meadow. Small groups of pines rear their tops a hundred feet and more above the grassy plain; their shade affords the most delightful camping grounds that can be desired. The lake itself is a placid, deep blue body of water, about two miles in circumference. It is navigated by several small row boats, and is well stocked with the most delicious fish, a variety of small trout, extremely sweet and palatable; when fried to a crisp there is nothing more relishing.

Families in search of health or tourists of pleasure need go no farther. There both are secured. The excursions that may be made from Silver Lake as headquarters are numerous and varied in their attractions. Bridle paths lead out in every direction; penetrating the narrow defiles that lead farther up towards the eminent snow-clad summits, they discover new beauties of scenery every mile. Lakes of various magnitude, studded with granite boulders of enormous size, for islands, lie closely girt within walls of adamant, whose precipitous cliffs reach to the skies above. Once upon the dividing summit of the Cottonwoods, American Fork and Wasatch County cañons, a marvel of glorious landscape greets the eye. Illimitable ranges of verdure-covered hills, relieved here and there with white glistening peaks spread out in all directions for miles around, while below an almost perfect circle is formed by the narrow, clear cut precipice which forms the dividing ridge. Within this circle a peak of granite raises aloft its venerable head. From the foundation depths of mother Earth it has come up to crown the wondrous works of Nature, and assert its patriarchal claim to be above all, as it is first of all in the formation of the globe. It is called Mount Eyrie; named by an adventurous and beautiful young lady, whose intrepidity led her to make its ascent. At the moment of reaching the top, and while thinking of a suitable name for the mount, an eagle rose from among the cliffs and, circling round above her head, seemed disposed to dispute the right of invasion of his eyrie home.

Down the Snake Creek gulch a few miles, the path turns and leads to the open valley of the Provo. Near the little town of Midway are springs of singular formation and great interest. The warm mineral waters containing the substances to compose their own enclosure, have sprung up, and flowing over the surface, have deposited, for generations past, the layers of lime sediment which now, heaped up in cones, completely wall in the deep wells of water, which are large enough for fine plunge baths, and even admit of swimming. In some of these curiously formed reservoirs the water has found an under current and disappeared, leaving them dry and open to relocation by the reptilian family. Several years ago the rattlesnakes of the neighborhood, taking advantage of this circumstance, took up their abode in one of these vacant wells or caves, as they came to be called, and there propagated largely, none daring to molest or make them afraid. On the occupation by settlers of the country around, the rendezvous of these dangerous neighbors was discovered, and warfare opened upon them. It took some time to entirely annihilate the hosts of venomous creatures that composed the colony; but finally the unrelenting arm of the white man, mostly cowboys, finished the work of extirpation, relieving the settlers of danger. A trip by horseback to these wells may be made from Silver Lake and return in a day.

Setting out in another direction, Bald Mountain may be crossed and the mines of Park City visited. It will be found a most enjoyable excursion, the scenery from the top of the mountain being very commanding and beautiful. A few years ago, a lady teacher of one of the city schools set forth upon this tour. She was well advanced in years, as lady teachers are, and of impaired eyesight; but she held to the abhorrence of men with the determination characteristic of her class. She had never seen the "mortal man" that could daunt her courage, which had marked out the solitary path of life she had chosen to pursue. Though Senators, Supreme Judges, and a defeated candidate for President had been at her feet, it was of no avail. Her resolution to live alone, teach and die had been taken, and no power should ever thwart her plans. Upon the journey she had undertaken to the Park she declined the companionship of any *man*, and there being no ladies to go with her, she strapped a long-necked bottle of strong tea to her shoulders, and with staff in hand, proceeded upon her journey, which was successfully performed, and the return commenced. As the level rays of the setting sun cast long shadows of trees and rocks over the barren sides of Bald Mountain, our heroine of the long-necked bottle (for so she became known) trudged lonely and happily on her way down the steep slope. The melancholy tingle of a distant cowbell was the only sound that broke the stillness of the departing day. Her soul was charmed with the sublimity of nature. There was nothing in all the landscape round that broke the harmony of her pure thoughts. She seemed wedded to nature. The reflection was delightful—herself and nature—alone. No man, no senator, no presidential candidate—but just herself and nature. Would that it might ever be thus! But a new element, gradually, like a myth, arose in the dim horizon of the perfect picture of peace that met the gaze of our fair lady. A stalwart form, the form of a god it seemed to her uncertain vision, grew upon the retina of her enraptured eye. Being so much enamored of nature, is it any wonder that one of nature's sons should break the spell, and win the heart that the civilized intrigue of cultivated man-made men had failed to conquer? Here stood before her a son of the mountains, clothed in buckskin, brown, rough, wild, grizzled, but a child of nature—a prospector—she loved him where he stood—he afterwards struck a lead and she married him. "Frailty thy name is woman!" *Amalric.*

CREATION AND PROGRESS.

THE lack of faith is one of the distinguishing traits of the age; one of its prominent sins. Yet, perhaps, it is hardly to be wondered at, considering how long and how often men have been deceived and befooled with false creeds and spurious gospels, that have had scarcely the form of Godliness, to say nothing of its power. This tendency to skepticism may be regarded as one of the natural results of the great apostacy, and its only cure is the preaching of the everlasting and unchangeable Gospel revealed in these last days. But even the preaching of the Gospel has indirectly had the tendency to increase this spirit of infidelity, for many who have heard its glad tidings but have not had sufficient honesty or courage to embrace it, have had their faith in their old dogmas and creeds so entirely shattered, that their only refuge and hiding place has been behind the dark platform of a system that teaches them that there is no God, no heaven, no hereafter, nothing but this present life, and that the material universe grew into existence by gradual development without a creator, and continues in all its beauty, harmony and perfection independent of a great all-wise governing power, or controlling hand. When men of thought, not entirely bound up in the traditions of the age, reject the Gospel as taught by the Church of Jesus Christ of Latter-day Saints, they reject Christianity, and have no place for the soles of their feet, except upon the platform of a vain philosophy which denies everything except what it claims to prove by reason and analogy, or in the mysticism of spiritualism or spiritism, which makes men credulous in all things, except in those principles that have their foundation in the revelations of God. To believe too much or believe too little, are both equally dangerous and liable to deceive the human mind in its search after the truth.

Some men claim that to believe in special creations, is to believe in miracles, or divergences from the well understood laws of nature, which miracles they arrogantly assert, they never see manifested in this stage of the earth's existence. But if they do not believe in the eternity of matter they must necessisarily believe in one special creation, however insignificant, to commence with, and if they believe in one, why not in many? Is it any more difficult, from a philosophical standpoint, to believe in many creations than in one? We think not, but it is much more philosophical to believe in the eternity of matter and that each species—animal, plant, etc., has from eternity been bearing seed in itself after its kind, as it does now. To believe this requires no acceptance of miracles, though a miracle, as a general thing, is simply a manifestation of the laws of nature somewhat different to that usually presented before the eyes of mankind, and as men do not comprehend it, they have ascribed to it the convenient name of miracle, or dubbed it supernatural. And while we sincerely believe in what are familiarly termed miracles, we have not the slightest faith that anything that could be legitimately called supernatural ever occurred. It is a misnomer, for all things in nature are subject to nature's unchangeable laws, and as nothing is a mystery to those who understand, so nothing is supernatural to those beings who comprehend all of nature's laws. The workings of electricity as seen in the telegraph, the telephone, etc., are far more miraculous than many occurences called by that name. But it is only the untutored savage that would consider the effects of electricity supernatural, for the simple reason that civilized man knows enough of its manifestations to understand that they are all governed by well ordered laws, many of which he has already discovered and applied, and others he is gradually unfolding.

There is very much false reasoning in the assumptions of those who deny the existence of the Divine Being. They ascribe effects to utterly inadequate causes. The difference between the intelligence and spiritual powers of man and those of the brute, they ascribe to difference in the size and structure of the brain, and the organs through which it works. Difference of structure is asserted to be the cause of difference of function, and man is simply an improved or more perfect animal than the beasts by which he is surrounded and whom he rules. But there is something more than difference of structure that causes the distinction between man and the brutes. It is difference of origin, difference of parentage and descent. Man was as inherently capable of the high attainments of to-day, had the surrounding circumstances been as favorable, in the earliest ages of this world's history, as he is now. There is no evidence of the gradual development of man as a race from the universal barbarism of the stone age to the enlightenment of the present. The theory of the gradual mental growth of the whole human family through the slow bronze, iron ages, etc., once so popular with those who did not want to believe the Scriptures, is fast falling into disrepute. There is nothing to prove the universal prevalence of any one state of society in any age of the world's history since the creation; whilst some nations were growing, others were retro-grading; it is so to day; it has been so ever since the nations divided, and the races of men commenced to work out their individual history. We know, that the Egyptian, the Persian, and the Lamanite are far below the standard of the civilization of their ancient ancestors, while other races are still growing and improving in all the excellencies of humanity.

Modern science is too much given to generalizing. It knows a little, and assumes everything. Let us suppose for a moment that every record relating to the history of Utah could be wiped out of existence, and two thousand years from now, philosophers of that age dig up some of the workmanship of our most skilled artizans, say some complicated machinery; then again, that others dig up some flint arrow heads or other rough work of our friends the Diggers, the Utes, or Shoshones, what could these parties know by deduction about our state of society? Would they not probably, according to the present system of reasoning, conclude that the arrow heads were the work of a people who antedated by many thousand years, the men who constructed the delicate pinions, or massive beams of the machinery, and argue that the one was the gradual development of the other, instead of being two diverse races occupying the same region at the same time. And then let us imagine they find the remains of Kit Carson's boat hewed out of a log, which is now in our Museum, by what process of reasoning, at present in vogue, could they ascribe it to one of the enlightened race. They must know the circumstances that surrounded the building of that boat before they could decide correctly. So is it with many of the relics of earlier ages of the world's history that are to day advertised as stumbling blocks to the revelations of the Bible. They prove but little, and amount to nothing when they are exhibited as evidences of the untrustworthiness of the Divine Record. True, they may disprove some of the theories advanced by uninspired men, which such pretend are based upon the Bible; but that is a matter between the scientists and theorizers, but these finds disprove none of God's revealed word, nor demonstrate that there is no creator, nor that the race of man was ever anything radically different to what it is to day, or ever developed or differentiated from one of the lower creations.   *R.*

CORRESPONDENCE.

CHIPPEWA FALLS, IOWA.

Editor Contributor:

If I can arrange my thoughts, and present my ideas on paper, I would like to tell the young men of Zion what qualifications are necessary to become good missionaries. I am aware that many of our Elders have had but limited education, yet, through the aid of the Spirit of God, have done much good on missions. But this is no excuse for us, who enjoy opportunities which they did not have; "where much is given, much is required," and it is our duty to get knowledge from all good books and all proper sources. Here let me say I consider the knowledge that comes from the Lord, through communion with His Spirit, is to be preferred before all other knowledge. First of all I would therefore recommend, as the greatest qualifier, simple, childlike prayer. Pray in faith. Let no young man think he will obtain and retain communion with the Father, unless he lives a life of virtue, a life of morality, a life of cleanliness and of temperate habits. "For my spirit dwells not in unholy tabernacles, saith the Lord."

These things having been observed, the next thing I would recommend is to become thoroughly conversant with the Bible, not only to repeat the various appropriate passages, but also to tell under what circumstances and conditions they were given. The Book of Mormon and Doctrine and Covenants should likewise be committed. Add to these, histories of the churches, the creeds and doctrines taught by other denominations. Go into your researches deep. Don't be satisfied with a mere glance. The more you have of real knowledge, the more you have to draw from; histories of great men and of nations are good; geography is essential; all true science will aid you. Then an understanding of music, sufficient, at least, to enable you to lead a hymn, is advantageous. Don't fail to embrace every opportunity of speaking in public, thus to accustom yourself to stand before an audience. And the young man that will make God his choice, keep the Word of Wisdom, and store his mind as I have advised, will be able, through the aid of the Lord, to stand before all men and not be confounded.

I write thus on account of the idea some have that it is not necessary to prepare themselves for missions, thinking, no doubt, that they will not be called. The field is large, and all who are qualified will be needed. We are told that whatever intelligence we attain unto in this life will rise with us in the life to come, and we believe no man can obtain a high exaltation in ignorance. That all my young brethren may improve the golden moments as they fly, and make of themselves skilled artizans in the work of God, is the desire of your friend and brother.   *Thomas J. Steed.*

HOMESPUN TALK.

THOUGHT you'd bring your boy friends with you, did you? That's right my dears. Here are seats. Glad you came in, I have just done my evening chores. Don't I dislike doing chores? Why, yes, of course I do, but I don't grumble about them. I do think if there is any thing on earth that is trying to patience it is for the different members of a family to neglect their chores. You see they are necessary evils. I don't want you to feel offended my dear boys, at what I say, but I am glad of an opportunity of giving you some much needed advice on this subject. I know its disagreeable to work all day and have to come home and milk, and chop wood, and feed stock, etc. But it has to be done, so do it cheerfully, as your mother or sister does hers. Suppose you have to say to your mother about eight or ten times, "I want my supper," "Sew on this button," or "make my bed," and then have to go and throw on the bed-clothes, hunt up something to eat or pin up your shirt collar. It is quite as trying for mother or wife to ask and ask for wood or water and then toil up the hill after the heavy bucket of water, or haggle off a stick of wood, or worse, pick up tantalizing chips in the hot sun. Do you think its fun for her! The doing of these same chores is the oil which lubricates the intricate machinery of domestic labor. And oh, when the wheels get dry how they do squeak? In fact I have known some to get so clogged that they moved slower and slower and finally stopped. A young man lately married, whose wife was possessed of good common sense, dropped into his old habit of neglecting chores as long as possible. One morning his wife wanted wood but he was engaged talking to some man about fields. The wife called several times and got the time honored reply, "Yes, my dear, in a minute." After a while the calls ceased, and the husband settled down with a sigh of relief on the top of a fence rail. The hour for breakfast came and in walked the young man. The table was set as usual. They sat down and he was helped to white unboiled potatoes, the plate of raw beefstake was by his side, and the table was crowned with a breadpan full of uncooked dough. We draw the curtain. Men get tired of chores, while a woman's life is made up of them, and like them or not they have to be done. And now, don't forget when you go home to-night to do up what few chores you may have to do cheerfully and well. Good night, come again. *Susa Young Gates.*

REAL AND IDEAL.

At times sweet visions float across my mind,
  And glimpses of the unknown bright and fair,
Where all the objects seem so well-defined—
  Tasteful in color, and in beauty rare,
That I must pause, and think if they be real,
Or only what the poets call ideal.

I well remember when a little child,
  I had these same strange, wand'ring fancies;
And I was told my thoughts were running wild,
  That I must not indulge in such romances,
Wasting in idle dreams the precious hours,
Building air-castles and gazing from the towers.

E'en then I seemed to familiar things,
  Pertaining to a dim, uncertain past;
And to my recollection faintly clings,
  A sense of something, which the shadows cast,
That showed me what my future life would be,
A prophecy, as 'twere, of destiny.

There was an intuition in my heart,
  An innate consciousness of right and wrong,
That bade me choose a wiser, better part,
  Which, in rough places, helped to make me strong;
And though my path was oft bereft of beauty,
Still urged me on to fulfil ev'ry duty.

O, happy childhood, bright with faith and hope,
  Enchantment dwells within thy rosy bowers,
And rainbow tints gild all within thy scope,
  And youth sits lightly on a bed of flowers,
His cup of happiness just brimming o'er,
Unconscious of what life has yet in store.

What glowing aspirations fill the mind—
  Of noble work designed for man to do!
What purity of purpose here we find—
  What longings for the beautiful and true;
Ere know we of the toil, the grief and woe;
Or dream that men and women suffer so.

Though all along life's weary, toilsome way,
  We meet with disappointments hard to bear,
Yet strength is given equal to our day,
  And joy is of 'nest mixed with pain and care;
But let us not grow weary in well-doing,
Still persevere the upward path pursuing.

Thus ever struggle on, 'mid doubts and fears,
  While changing scenes before our gaze unfold,
Till, through the vista of long, weary years,
  We see heav'n's sunshine, thro' its gates of gold;
And feel assured it is an answering token,
Aye! though our earthly idols have been broken.

Tho' those we've cherish'd most have been untrue,
  And fond and faithful ones have gone before,
Still let us keep the promises in view,
  Of those who're pleading on "the other shore,"
Whose tender messages are with us yet,
The words of love, we never can forget.

And while we muse and ponder, shadows fall,
  And a sweet spirit whispers, "Peace, be still;"
What of the past—'tis now beyond recall;
  The future, we with usefulness may fill.
Yet sometime, we shall find in regions real
Those dreams fulfilled we only term ideal.
        Emmeline B. Wells.

THE CONTRIBUTOR.

A MONTHLY MAGAZINE.

JUNIUS F. WELLS,
EDITOR AND PUBLISHER.

TERMS:
Two Dollars a Year,   -   In Advance.
Single Copy, Twenty Cents.

SALT LAKE CITY,   JULY, 1881.

SECTARIAN SCHOOLS.

THERE has been of late, considerable said in the stand and by the press upon sectarian schools among the Latter-day Saints. In our comments upon this subject, we desire to take the correct view and to weigh the situation fairly and without prejudice.

That there is universal sectarian opposition to our people and institutions none will deny. There is no church, no society, no political party of the world that favors the Saints. A few years ago, all of them that were not actively engaged in the assault, remained at home in indifference, at ease, while our people were being driven from the pale of civilization, their leaders murdered and their homes destroyed. While these atrocities were being committed, and a friendless people ostracised from their native land, none of these good Christians, whose mission is to educate poor children and send missionaries to the heathen, were known to pen a line, deliver a sermon or raise an arm in defense of the helpless Saints, or in opposition to the cruel bigotry and relentless frenzy that actuated the mobs who drove them into the wilderness.

Now, with these historical facts before us, we have to conclude that the solicitude at present manifested by the sectarian Christians of the world, in behalf of the youth of the Latter-day Saints, is the result of a change of sentiment in regard to our people, or it is to be viewed in the light of a new invasion, with the same fell purpose that the mobs had in Missouri and Illinois, namely, the destruction of our faith and people.

If we ask the ministers the object of their extreme interest, they commence to generalize. Education is their theme, broad, liberal education, that will make refined, intelligent men and women of our children. This, they say, to us, is the first and only consideration they have in view, and they spend their time and devote their strength and talent to its accomplishment for the love of Christ and humanity, being sustained, in the meantime, by the church funds and school perquisites, tuition fees, etc. It is hard for some of us Latter-day Saints to believe that they have no other object or intention; that they do not wish to destroy our children's faith in our religion; and that purely for the love they bear us, they are willing to educate our children without money and without price. We are made more incredulous when we read the dispatches, and find that our anxious educators humiliate themselves, begging money in the east to support them in the glorious cause of education among the Mormons, and that to raise sufficient interest and money they are obliged to waive the matter of truth and greatly exaggerate the extent of their field, and the necessity of its thorough cultivation.

Our faith, in the innocent nature of their calling, and in the purity of their designs upon our children, is further wrecked, when we hear that they tell other stories of their purposes and objects to their patrons abroad. They say that a famous bishop of one of the leading sectarian churches here, told his fellow bishops in Boston, that he could do nothing towards converting the adult Mormons to the popular creeds, for they were rooted and grounded in their delusion, but "in ten years you will see we will make great inroads upon their children." His remarks were applauded. Remarks like this, and their bitter denunciation of our Church leaders and some of the principles of our faith, which they compare to diabolism, animalism, etc., necessarily cause thinking Latter-day Saints to suspect that "there's a nigger in the fence" somewhere.

Now, what *is* the design and object of

sectarian churches in seeking to educate Latter-day Saints' children? They say, "we do not teach religion in our schools. Your children may or may not be Presbyterians, Episcopalians, or Methodists. It is our business simply to give them a common or high school education; not to interfere with their religion, whatever it may be." But with their ideas of Mormonism, viewing it as evil, abominable, immoral, and not orthodox, what kind of men must they be, and how will they account to their supporters East, if they make no effort to destroy the germ of faith in the breasts of Mormon children, which is sure to develop into a perfect testimony of the truth of Mormonism if left alone?

They are hypocrites and false to their trust if they do not seek to dispel from the minds of children under their care, any theories, or principles not in accord with their traditional ideas of Christianity, morality, and respectability. And any one of them, not believing in Mormonism, who would assume to teach a Mormon child, and not correct in the mind of that child, the principles its parents, as good Latter-day Saints, are bound to impart, is too much of a hypocrite to his own faith, to be trustworthy or fit to teach, guide or control any one, and particularly children of whom great things are expected in the future.

These teachers *have* some other object in view, and are doing what they consider a nobler work than merely instructing our children in grammar and arithmetic. The arithmetic they take most delight in teaching, and which they expect the greatest results from, is *infidelity to Mormonism.* Certainly we wont insist on you being Baptists or Congregationalists, or even Catholics, so that you are anything under heaven but a Mormon. The devil is well enough satisfied with the victory, and is willing to let his various sectarian churches clamber among themselves for the spoils.

We consider that Latter-day Saints' children have a claim upon their parents for a fair education. They are the offspring of a system that the world abhors, and they have to contend for a place in the world with their fellow men arrayed, on every hand, against them. To be prepared for the battle of life, to be able to defend their father's faith and to give a reason for the hope within them, they must be educated. They must be able to meet the theologian, the scientist, the philosopher, and confute strange theories and vindicate the truth. For this labor they should be educated. They have a wonderful mission upon the earth, and should be trained from childhood directly and purposely for its fulfillment. Neglect of parents to start them well drilled, armed and in condition to meet the opponents of their life's mission, will be visited upon the parents' heads. If the youth fall by the wayside, skeptics, unvirtuous, infidel, let parents take warning. Where have the little ones been taught? If in the school of the unbeliever, their sin be upon your heads. If in the school of faith, God will visit His judgments upon them and recompense you for the care you have given them.

In most cases where the latter course is pursued, there will be little danger of children going astray. "Train up a child in the way he should go, and when he is old he will not depart from it" is a true saying. The only difficulty is in knowing how he should go and training him accordingly. If Latter-day Saints do not know the destiny and expectations of their children, they certainly can not suppose sectarian school teachers to be better informed. We are of the opinion that children, with the work before them that our children have to do, deserve better treatment than to be subjected to the false traditions and infidel influences of bigoted sectarians, before they have learned the whisperings of the Holy Spirit which God gave them in their early childhood, to be their monitor and help, while obtaining their education. And we consider it an insult to those children, if not an offense to God, for parents to place them where the development and employment of that sacred gift is not deemed necessary to educate and qualify them for the duties of life which await them.

Therefore, if parents desire and expect to have joy in their posterity, let them take the course which will secure it. From the time that their little ones are old enough to discern the influences of good and evil, make it obligatory upon those who teach them, to inculcate reverence for the former; thereby developing acquaintance with the spirit of intelligence and truth, that the Lord has implanted within them to be their guide and director through the life they are sent here to live. The results will justify the care.

OUR SOCIETY.

To be a good member of a "Mutual Improvement Association," implies, that there is a determination to improve, and also a settled purpose to use all the opportunities which such Society gives, that the improvement may be secured.

And to improve, each one must understand and know his own peculiar defects. His own personal criticism, as he has opportunities of contrast, will enable him to see more and more plainly where he needs to cultivate, or seek to improve. In listening to a good reader, a poor one discovers how much he lacks in this particular; in hearing a good, ready, fluent speaker, one who is not so feels his imperfection; although there may be fluency without any great manifestation of intelligence, if you couple the two together, fluency and the evidences of thought, ignorance and inability feel at once that they have room for improvement. When a rude and selfish person comes in contact with one who is well behaved, kind in heart and spirit, and studious of the feelings of others, he is a rebuke to the vain and forward, to the rude and unpolished, the thoughtless of man or womankind. Those whose language is vulgar and uncouth, who use slang phrases, swear and take the name of God in vain, are never so much abashed, nor realize their vulgarity, as when in the society of those who are refined in manner, and who, in language full of simplicity and music, express their feelings or their wants.

There is no rebuke so effectual with the skeptic, as the unfaltering trust in God and faith in His providences, which Saints exhibit when trial and sorrow throw a shadow across their line of life. It is the integrity of the Saints, their devotion to the cause they have espoused which arouses the raillery and inspires the opposition of the enemy. But every well disposed person turns mid these contrasts of life to the brighter—the better side; to the path of improvement, of progress, of education, of refinement, of increased intelligence and consequent power in this life and in the life to come. The members of our Associations should mark all the most desirable qualities which they see exhibited by others, and then seek to emulate these examples, improving in reading, in singing, in composition or writing, in expression as in speaking, in behavior and conduct towards all around them, in ability to think on religious things, on things which are called secular, such as business matters, social matters, and domestic matters, constantly enlarging their sphere of thought and adding to their stores of knowledge; gathering a little here, a little there, an item from one, a hint from another, and a thought from the next, so "Improvement" will not be a catchword only, but a real, living, accomplished thing. How much more companionable, how much more useful, how much more manly and womanly, nay even how much more God-like might our youth become, if they were but a little more earnest in their desire and search for "Mutual Improvement;" acting upon and also being acted upon by others, supplanting ignorance by intelligence; error by truth; poverty of thought by reflection in many directions; rudeness and vulgarity by cultivation and good manners; indifference to God and His worship, by a living faith and abiding testimony; the following of gentile fashions, by the simplicity of attire as inculcated in the gospel; indulgence in all the stimulants used to the dethronement of reason, the destruction of vital force and the shortening of human life, by a steadfast obedience to every "Word of Wisdom," and the ushering in of such renovating processes as shall favorably affect longevity, until man shall again "Live to the age of a tree;" in other words, overthrowing every institution and influence which in their origin are but of man, and establishing those institutions and spreading those influences which are divine; thus recognizing God and righteousness as the fountain and stream, from whence for "The healing of the nations," and the realization of all the dreams of mutual improvement that can ever come to Saint or sinner in this probation, or indeed, in any other sphere, where agency purified and enobled by experience and intelligence, shall aspire to the society and glory of the Gods!

Industrious use of all the faculties, mid all the opportunities of life, with a reverential yet earnest seeking for the power of the Holy Ghost, (which is an everpresent inspiration) will enable every member of both sexes, of this and kindred associations to become mighty in the arena of "Mutual Improvement;" aiding ourselves, aiding each other, and aiding the building of the Kingdom of God through that Priesthood, whose watchword is "Onward," and whose lever is and has been "Mutual Improvement."

H. W. Naisbitt.

HINTS ON PREACHING.

THE great and important duty of preaching the Gospel is of such vital moment, especially in this the last dispensation, that the Elders to whom the labor is entrusted should certainly be willing at all times to take into consideration how they can most effectually perform it to the acceptance of Heaven, and to the salvation of the souls of men. Human nature is pretty much the same all over the world, as regards its main features, attributes and propensities. Conciliatory measures are generally more acceptable, and consequently more successful, than the opposite, in removing prejudice, and promoting confidence and faith in the doctrine to be advanced. An open warfare need not be declared against the present convictions of an audience, in order to institute a more acceptable and truthful standard of Gospel life and practice. To give a congregation to understand that you mistrust their honesty of heart, their integrity of purpose, or their sound common sense, even if such were actually the case, would not be calculated to arouse the most pleasant reflections, nor to mould their minds into the most congenial humor for receiving the truths we have to offer for their acceptance. On the contrary, to apparently agree with them on minor and unimportant points, to go with them as far as the tenor of their road leads towards our destination, will better prepare them for going with us, part way at least, when the roads diverge. It is an old axiom, that "if you go with your companion to the forks of the road, you can then take him whithersoever you will."

To figuratively fight and oratorically cudgel an assembly, would hardly be considered the more certain method of allaying their antagonism to your doctrine, but rather to engender a dislike to the speaker, and through him, a contempt for his principles. A liberality of sentiment concerning the opinions of others, erroneous as they may be, will always induce a greater sympathy towards our own. There is probably nothing so repulsive to an audience as a dogmatical address: an effort to coerce the public mind to our way of thinking by arrogant assertion, instead of convincing by argument, persuading by appeals to reason, and touching the heart by the sweet spirit of inspiration. The warfare of the Gospel is not waged against men, but against error; and all its administrations are characterized by love for the human race, who are the offspring of God. Its mission is to supplant ignorance by revealing knowledge, to cultivate acceptance of that which is good and true by showing its beauty and consistency.

The mind intuitively reverences that which is holy. The divine in man responds to the divine in principle, when advanced by an inspired speaker. Love begets love. But few there are who will not recognize kindness, and yield to a loving appeal to their hearts or reason, in preference to an attack upon their ignorance, wilfulness or stupidity. Notwithstanding the latter may be most apparent, still wisdom suggests that much should be ignored in the effort to infuse correct principle into a benighted, traditionated and prejudiced mind.

Another thing that should be regarded is: in all our arguments, we should hold the fact prominently before the people, that God has revealed this Gospel from heaven; that it is for this reason it should be believed, rather than that we ourselves are convinced of its Scriptural correctness, or that our investigations have been more profound or our conclusions more just than others. Intelligent audiences do not like to be made to believe a doctrine simply because the preacher is convinced, without hearing the "strong reasons" which induced him to believe. Neither do they always regard his opinion as paramount, because he may claim to have stood well in the community. He may, however, show what opportunities he has had for investigation of the subject in hand. Apt quotations from historical information found in his researches, will always interest and edify, as well as make a point in his argument. People naturally like to hear brief incidents narrated, the truth of which is established by some historical record. These, however, should be made as concise as possible, and directly to the point. Arguments lose force and effect, if we stray off from the subject to tell an out of place story. The hottest iron will "cool off" if the

smith stops beating to go out and see a "dog fight." The minds of the audience should be kept intensely interested in our subject; and in order to effect this, their sympathy must be engaged. Illustrations best adapted to meet their own experiences should be used to portray any given idea, and if metaphors are introduced, let them by all means be appropriate and telling. We should never speak for the purpose of display. The individual who yields to this flimsy temptation defeats his own object. It deprives his efforts of that fervor—that warmth of self-conviction, and that earnest desire for the salvation of his hearers which are such aids to the preacher in making converts. Hence the telling effects of a strong testimony to the Gospel, showing not merely belief in the doctrine, but positive revealed knowledge concerning its truth. People may not always believe through hearing our testimony, but they may be led to an investigation and further inquiry into a doctrine so forcibly advanced and sustained. Furthermore, it is our duty to testify of that which we *do know* concerning this great work, that those who will not heed our teaching may at last have to face our testimony; and thus, by having every opportunity of conversion, be left without excuse before the judgment seat of God.

On the manner of preaching the Gospel, we find a commandment of the Lord, published on the one hundred and twentieth page of the Book of Doctrine and Covenants (n.e.), in a revelation to Martin Harris, given in March, 1830, through Joseph the Seer: "And thou shalt declare glad tidings, yea, publish it upon the mountains, and upon every high place, among the people that thou shalt be permitted to see. *And thou shalt do it with all humility, trusting in Me, reviling not against revilers. And of tenets thou* SHALT NOT *talk, but thou shalt declare repentance and faith on the Savior, and remission of sins by baptism and by fire, yea, even the Holy Ghost.* Behold, this is a great and the last commandment which I shall give you concerning this matter; for this shall suffice for thy daily walk, even unto the end of thy life. And misery thou shalt receive if thou wilt slight these counsels; *yea, even the destruction of thyself and property.*"

How plainly does · this endorse the principle which is the subject of our article! Here is a direct command not to "talk of tenets," showing that attacks upon religious creeds are in the very nature of things calculated to arouse the worst kind of opposition, for Martin Harris was positively warned that misery should come upon him if he slighted these counsels; and that it would end in the destruction of himself and property.

The Gospel revealed from Heaven is so broad and deep and high, that it furnishes ample scope for preaching, without spending time in analysing and attacking the systems of religion that surround us; and when it is preached in the power and demonstration of the Holy Spirit, its comparative beauties will be apparent to the honest seeker after truth. Let him make his own comparison between the Gospel revealed through Joseph and the creed which he has hitherto believed as divine, and we doubt not the result will be manifest in due time. By taking this course, the speaker will stimulate and promote the healthy action of the hearer's mind, will thus draw upon his good sense instead of arousing his combativeness; and his heart, touched as it were, by the magic wand of eternal truth, yields willing obedience to the behests of Heaven, and blesses the hand that wielded it for his salvation.—*Millennial Star.*

A HOMILY ON VICE.

VICE is the extreme opposite of virtue, or virtue violated. Great vices, like great virtues, are not the creation of a day or an hour, but come by the repetition of little acts in our everyday life, as we journey on. Our words and our actions are but the echo of the mind; if our minds are occupied by evil and corrupt thoughts, they will, by persistent indulgence, create habits of life and vices that will bring us to shame and destruction.

When a young man first launches out into the world, he sees some people who shine, and who seem to be admired and esteemed; he discovers, on acquaintance, that they carry many vices, that they are genteel drunkards, gamblers, etc., upon which he adopts their way of living, mistaking their defects for their perfections, and thinking that they owe their lustre to those genteel vices, whereas it is exactly the reverse; for they have acquired their good reputation by their parts, their learning, their good breeding, and other real accomplishments, and are blemished and lowered in the opinion of all reasonable people, and of their own, in time, by their vices, which at first appear essential to their splendor.

Vanity, the source of many of our follies, and of some of our crimes, has sunk many a man into company in every light infinitely below himself, for the sake of being the first man in it. There he dictates, and is applauded, admired; and, for the sake of being the Coryphæus of that wretched chorus, disgraces and disqualifies himself soon for any better company. Depend upon it, you will sink or rise to the level of the company which you commonly keep; people will judge of you, and not unreasonably, by that. There is good sense in the Spanish saying, "Tell me whom you live with, and I will tell you who you are." Therefore, be extremely careful in the selection of companions. The adoption of vice has, I am convinced, ruined ten times more young men than natural inclinations. When a man considers the state of his own mind, he will find that the best defence against vice is preserving the worthiest part of his own spirit pure from any great offence against it. There is then a magnanimity in him which makes him look upon himself with disdain, if he is ever betrayed by a sudden desire or temptation, into the gratification of lust, covetousness, rage or pride.

If a man would preserve his own spirit, and his natural approbation of higher and more worthy pursuits, he could never fall into this littleness, but his mind would be still open to honor and virtue in spite of infirmities and relapses. Every step that a man takes beyond moderate and reasonable provision for his interests in any direction, is taking so much from the worthiness of his own spirit; as he that is entirely set upon making a fortune, is all that while undoing the man. He must grow deaf to the wretched, estrange himself from the agreeable, learn hardness of heart, disrelish everything that is noble, and terminate all in his dispicable self. Indulgence in any one immoderate desire or appetite engrosses the whole creature, and his life is sacrificed to that one desire or appetite; but how much otherwise is it with those that preserve alive in them something that adorns their condition, and shows the man, whether a prince or a beggar, above his fortune.

It is necessary to an easy and happy life, to possess our minds in such a manner as to be always well satisfied with our own reflections. The way to this state is to measure our actions by our opinions, and not by those of the rest of the world. The sense of other men might prevail over us in things of less consideration, but not in concerns where truth and honor are engaged.

John A. Hellstrom.

PUBLICATIONS RECEIVED.

THE COMPARATIVE EDITION OF THE NEW TESTAMENT. Both Versions in one book. Published by Porter & Coates, Philadelphia, and for sale by James Dwyer, Salt Lake City. Price, cloth extra, $1.50.

This is a very neat and handy edition of the new translation, showing in opposite columns the two versions, which may readily be compared as one reads. Of the new version a great deal may be said in its favor, but we are of the opinion that it will be many years before it will be generally adopted, and not then fully, as it at present reads. Perhaps when the learned translators who are engaged on the Old Testament complete their labors, some of the popular objections to certain passages of the New may be considered and the version improved accordingly. We would be glad to see the Bible text in every respect rendered according to the original, but until men inspired by the spirit in which it was written, shall undertake its revision we shall view the efforts of classical scholars with a degree of apprehension and doubt.

CAMPBELL'S HAND-BOOK OF [SYNONYMS AND PREPOSITIONS. For sale at Jos. H. Parry's Book Store. Price 50 cents.

This is a handy reference book for writers. It contains forty thousand words, and is so simply arranged that the right word in the right place can always be found on consulting it.

LA POLIGAMIA MORMONA Y LA MONOGAMIA CRISTIANA COMPARADAS. A defense of Polygamy, written and published in Spanish, by Elder Moses Thatcher, Mexico.

This is a very ably prepared pamphlet which shows from Scriptural, Philosophical and Natural Laws, the superiority of the Divine Law of Plurality of Wives, over the man made monogamic system of modern Christendom.

Spanish scholars of this city state that the work has been most carefully and excellently prepared. It must therefore take its place among the writings of the inspired servants of God, and its testimony stand as a witness against those who cannot be reached by other means.

WILD FLOWERS OF DESERET. By Augusta Joyce Crocheron. Published at *Juvenile Instructor Office.* Price, Leather, $1.50.

This is a new collection of poetic writings, by one of the most talented of our home poets. Mrs. Crocheron's contributions to the *Woman's Exponent,* to whose Editor she dedicates her book, have won for her the interest and affection of many readers, who will greet her beautiful little volume with delight. The "wild flowers" that are strewn upon its pages are varied in their color and fragrance, and will entertain and refresh not only the dwellers in Deseret, but many who live beyond the guardian ranges of our "hidden desert land."

Silence is just as far from being wisdom as the rattle of an empty wagon is from being music.

CPSIA information can be obtained
at www.ICGtesting.com
Printed in the USA
BVHW041258271218
536331BV00048B/695/P